PLANETS
and the
SOLAR SYSTEM

Troll Associates

PLANETS
and the
SOLAR SYSTEM

by Keith Brandt

Illustrated by Joseph Veno

Troll Associates

Library of Congress Cataloging in Publication Data

Brandt, Keith, (date)
    Planets and the solar system.

    Summary: Describes our solar system, which is made
up of nine planets, including Earth, which orbit
around the sun.
    1. Planets—Juvenile literature. 2. Solar system—
Juvenile literature. [1. Planets. 2. Solar system]
I. Veno, Joseph, ill. II. Title.
QB602.B68   1985   523.2   84-2714
ISBN 0-8167-0300-0 (lib. bdg.)
ISBN 0-8167-0301-9 (pbk.)

Imagine you are drifting in space. You see the sun and everything that travels around it. There are nine planets, each one different from all the rest. Our Earth is one of them. Around some of the planets you see moons or rings or clouds.

You also see balls of frozen gas called comets. They glow as they streak through space around the sun. There are also odd-shaped rocky objects that circle the sun just the way planets do. They are called asteroids. And there are smaller pieces of metallic rock that are called meteoroids. All of these objects in space—the sun, planets, moons, asteroids, meteoroids, and comets—make up our solar system.

The sun is at the center of our solar system. It is a great ball of very hot gas. The sun sends energy to Earth and to all the other planets. When we see light and feel heat, it is because of the sun's energy. The sun also has a strong pulling force called gravity. This gravity keeps the planets in their paths around the sun. If there were no solar gravity, each planet would fly off in a straight path into space.

Since ancient times people have been fascinated by the solar system. They watched the planets move through the sky and gave each one a name.

Sun

10

The fastest-moving planet is called Mercury, in honor of the swift messenger of the ancient Roman gods. Mercury is the planet closest to the sun. Because of this, the temperature on Mercury is very hot. During the day, it gets as hot as the broiler in a kitchen oven.

The surface of Mercury is dry and seems to be covered by craters, like our moon.

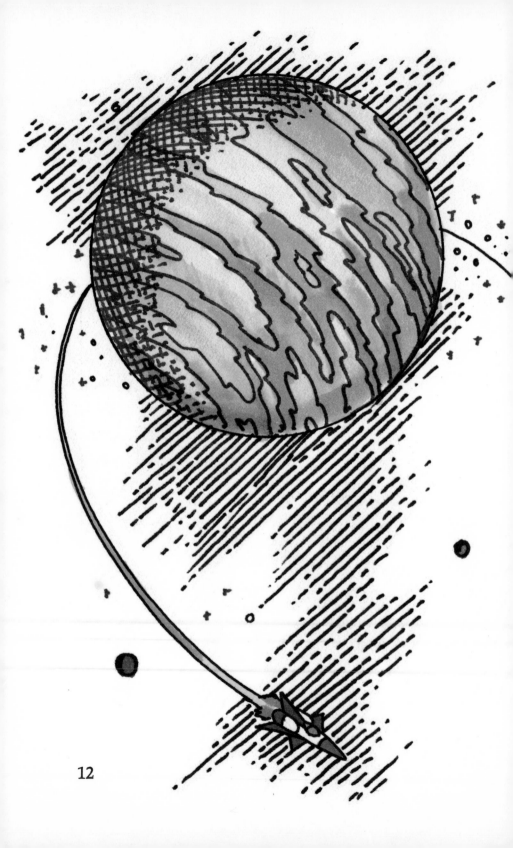

The second planet from the sun is named Venus, in honor of the Roman goddess of love and beauty. Venus is sometimes called the Morning Star or the Evening Star. That is because we see it shining brightly only at sunrise and sunset.

Venus has a thick, yellow atmosphere made of several gases, including nitrogen, carbon dioxide, argon, and water vapor. This atmosphere is so thick that we cannot see the planet's surface, even with our strongest telescopes. But scientists say it is very hot, dry, and dusty. The average temperature on Venus is about 800 degrees Fahrenheit.

The third planet from the sun is the Earth. It is the only planet in our solar system believed to support life as we know it. Our atmosphere, called air, is made up mostly of nitrogen and oxygen. On the surface of the Earth, there is plenty of water. It is the water on the Earth and the oxygen in the air that make life on this planet possible.

Earth

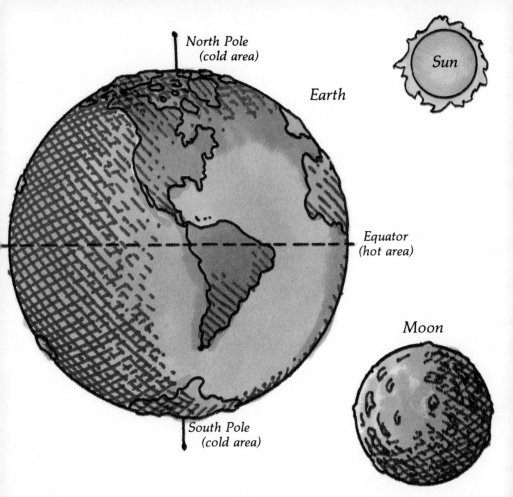

There are cold and hot places on our planet, but on most of the Earth, the temperature does not reach extremes. That is another reason why life flourishes on the Earth. Our planet has one natural satellite called the moon.

Mars, named for the Roman god of war, is the fourth planet from the sun. Because of its color it is also called the "red planet." The surface is rocky, dusty, and dry, although it has great ice caps at the poles.

Mars has a thin atmosphere that is mostly carbon dioxide, with small amounts of nitrogen, argon, and oxygen. It is very cold on Mars. The average temperature is about 80 degrees below zero Fahrenheit. Mars has two small satellites, called Phobos and Deimos.

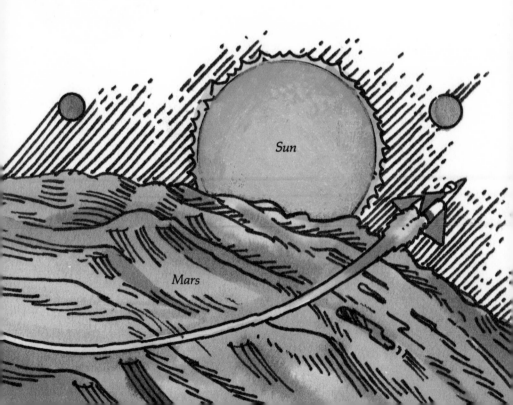

Sun

Mars

Jupiter, the fifth planet from the sun, is the biggest of all the planets. This huge planet has a very faint ring around it, plus sixteen moons. The moon called Io, which is the closest one to Jupiter, is known to have active volcanoes on its surface.

The surface of Jupiter, however, cannot be seen from Earth because of the thick clouds that surround the planet. Scientists believe that Jupiter has an incredibly hot core about the size of the Earth. Around this core is a great mass of liquid hydrogen and helium.

Above the planet's liquid surface is a violently stormy cover of clouds. Great orange and white bands of clouds race past each other in opposite directions, creating hurricane-like storms that last for years. Lightning crackles through the whirling layers of atmosphere, which may contain crystals of ice and ammonia, as well as hydrogen and helium gas. In spite of the high temperature of the planet itself, the temperature at the top of Jupiter's cloud cover is extremely cold.

Io (satellite)

Saturn, the sixth planet from the sun, looks quite spectacular because of its rings. For many years, scientists thought there were only five or six rings. But space probes have sent back close-up pictures that show hundreds—perhaps thousands—of rings! They are almost like the grooves of a gigantic phonograph record, whirling around the huge, multi-colored planet.

The ring particles are probably made of ice or ice-covered rock. They may be held in place by some of Saturn's moons. We know of more than twenty moons that orbit Saturn. The temperature on Saturn may be 240 degrees below zero Fahrenheit. Its atmosphere, like that of Jupiter, is made of many bands of stormy clouds.

Uranus, Neptune, and Pluto are the seventh, eighth, and ninth planets from the sun. Uranus has five moons and at least nine rings. Neptune has two moons and may also have a ring system. Pluto, the smallest planet, has one moon. Future space probes may send back more information about surface features and any gases that may surround these faraway planets.

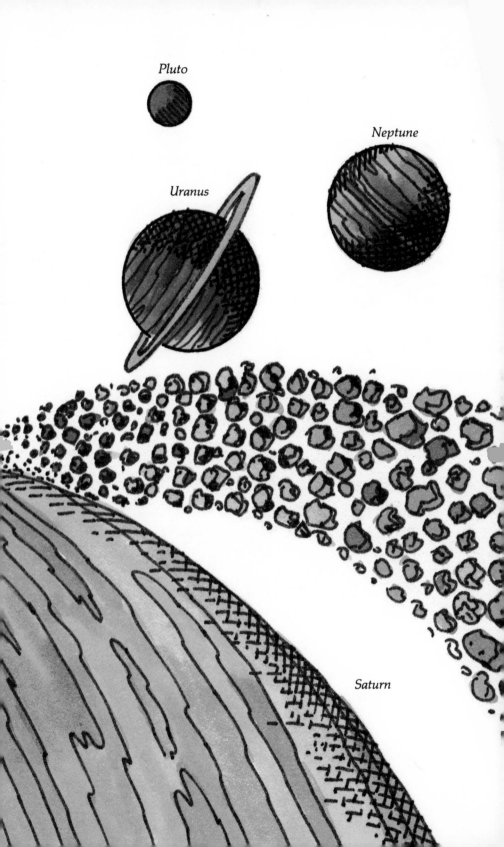

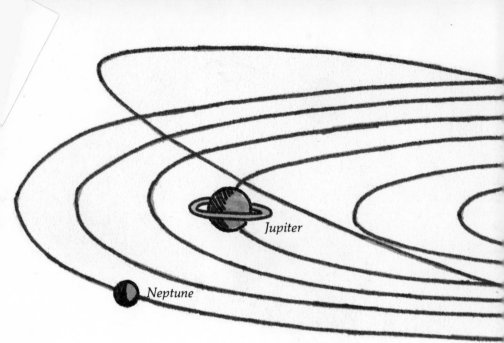

Jupiter

Neptune

All nine planets of the solar system travel around the sun in paths called orbits. The time it takes a planet to make one complete orbit—like a runner circling a track one time—is called a year. Earth takes a little more than 365 days to orbit the sun. That is how long Earth's year is.

Mercury is the planet closest to the sun, and it has the shortest orbit. So Mercury has the shortest year of all the planets. There are four years on Mercury for every Earth-year.

Pluto is farthest from the sun. So Pluto has the largest orbit in our solar system. One year on Pluto is longer than 250 Earth-years.

While each planet is orbiting the sun, it also does something else. It rotates, or spins like a top. This rotation makes night and day. When one side of Earth is facing the sun, it is day on that side. At the same time, it is night on the other side of Earth, where the sun's rays cannot reach. One complete rotation of the Earth takes twenty-four hours.

Each planet rotates at a different speed. Venus has the slowest rotation. In the time it takes for Venus to rotate once, the Earth rotates 243 times! Jupiter rotates fastest. One complete rotation for Jupiter takes less than ten hours.

Everything in the universe is moving all the time. The moon rotates as it orbits Earth. Earth rotates as it orbits the sun. The sun rotates as it moves endlessly through space.

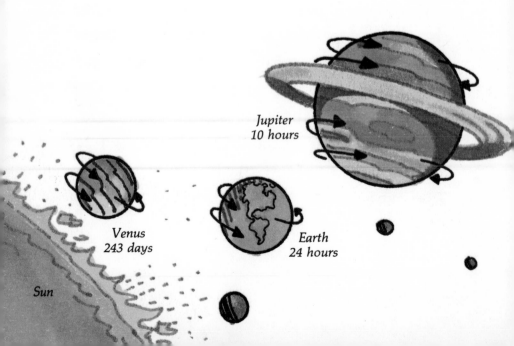

Jupiter
10 hours

Venus
243 days

Earth
24 hours

Sun

The solar system is more than four and a half billion years old. Nobody knows for sure how the solar system came to be. Some scientists think that the sun and planets were all formed from a single, flat cloud of gas.

Other scientists think that the planets were formed when a long stream of gas was pulled from the sun by the gravity of some huge passing object. Then gravity slowly pulled the gas together until the planets were formed. One thing we do know, however, is that the solar system stays together because of gravity.

In ancient times people did not know about gravity. Early astronomers studied the stars, but they did not have telescopes. So their ideas about the solar system came from what they could see with their eyes. They saw the sun rise and set every day. They saw the moon rise and set every night. They saw the stars slowly change their positions in the sky. So they thought that the Earth was the center of the universe.

But this did not explain everything they saw in the sky. It did not explain why planets sometimes seemed to move backwards or to stop moving altogether.

Then an astronomer named Ptolemy, who lived in ancient Egypt, came up with an explanation. He said that each planet moved in its own circle at the same time as it orbited Earth. And as the planets moved in their own circles, they only *seemed* to stop or to move backwards.

Many centuries went by before someone offered a better explanation. This person was a Polish astronomer named Copernicus. He said that the sun was the center of the solar system and that the Earth and all the other planets orbited around the sun.

Most people did not believe Copernicus. Then the telescope was invented, and an Italian astronomer named Galileo used it to prove that Copernicus was right.

Years later Isaac Newton, an English scientist, added to our knowledge of the solar system. He invented a more powerful

telescope to give us a clearer view of the heavens. He also worked out the very important theory called the law of gravity. It explained why planets stay in their orbits around the sun instead of flying off into space. It also explained why the moon stays in its orbit around Earth.

Today we know a great many things about the solar system. That is because we have very large telescopes to scan the skies, and very powerful instruments that pick up all kinds of scientific information from our solar system.

Space exploration teaches us many things. Astronauts have explored the moon. Space probes have sent us close-up photographs of Venus, Mars, Jupiter, and Saturn. Other probes have been sent out toward the most distant planets.

So far, the information sent back to Earth shows no signs of life as we know it on other planets in our solar system. But there are millions of other solar systems in the huge universe. Maybe there are planets like Earth in some of those solar systems. And maybe on one of those planets in some faraway solar system, there is intelligent life. What a marvelous discovery that would be!